# COUNTERPOINT

# Also available

# COUNTERPOINT

## R.S. THOMAS

BLOODAXE BOOKS

60074

ISBN: 1 85224 116 0 hardback edition
       1 85224 117 9 paperback edition

First published 1990 by
Bloodaxe Books Ltd,
P.O. Box 1SN,
Newcastle upon Tyne NE99 1SN.

Bloodaxe Books Ltd acknowledges
the financial assistance of Northern Arts.

Typesetting by Bryan Williamson, Darwen, Lancashire.

Printed in Great Britain by
Billing & Sons Limited, Worcester.

# BC.

This page should be left blank:
snow where the abominable footprints
have not yet appeared; sand
for the pioneer to stare over
in his questioning of the horizon.
What were its contents prior
to creation by divine mind?
And where did the viruses come from?

If you can imagine a brow puckered
before thought, imagine this page
immaculately conceived
in the first tree, with man rising
from on all fours endlessly to begin
puckering it with his language.

No, in the beginning was silence
that was broken by the word
forbidding it to be broken.

Hush: the sound of a bird landing
on water; sound of a thought
on time's shore; practice of Ur-language

by the first human. An echo
in God's mind of a conceived
statement. The sound of a rib

being removed out of the side
of the androgynous hero. The mumbling
of the Host by reptilian

lips. The shivering of love's
mirror as truth's frost
begins mercilessly to take hold.

It was a time when sparrows
lifted their voices above
the nightingales. The lonely
ones sang to their

aloneness; the audiences
were the sparrows'. Autumn
arrived; the nightingales
migrated. The sparrows died off

in their myriads. The frost
chirruped in places
where they had sat fast. From
bone galleries the audiences

had gone. In the hot south
featherless shadows fell
upon ruined cities that had never
heard the nightingales sing.

Of course there was no serpent.
The tree's fruit was a mirror,
its temptation reflection.

There is no Trinity
in a glass. The self looks at the self
only and tenders its tribute.

Who can read God's mind?
Was it two mirrors echoing
one another? And was the Holy
Spirit the breath clouding them
unable to discover
precedence in derivation
from the origin and the image,
perplexities of Nicaea?

What is the virginity
of mirrors? Are they surfaces
of fathoms which mind
clouds when examining itself
too closely? Eden in the dream
of when it was alone.

That was life's mischief
to create a plough
with no arable for it;
a chair without

a professor; twins the product
of no womb; a glittering
hunter but in need of
a quarry. And all as though

over our heads. Wiser
the Buddha who, though he looked
long, had no name for the packed
bud never to become a flower.

This at the bottom
of the ladder; Jacob wrestled
to no end. It was not
his name he withheld

but his number, that
atomic weight which decrees
when love is divided by love
there is no remainder.

I know him.
He is the almost anonymous,
the one with the near perfect
alibi, the face over us that lacks
nothing but an expression.
He is the shape in the mist
on the mountain we would ascend
disintegrating as we compose it.

He can outpace us
in our pursuit, outdistancing
time only to disappear
in a black hole. He acknowledges
our relationship in the modes of thought
repudiating, when we would embody
thought in language, a syntactical
compulsion to incorporate
him in the second person.

If he had not given them stone
how could they have begun building?

Without his shadow to measure his height
by Babel would have been a word long.

Does a God sleep? On that first night
the stars blinked ubiquitously as his eyelids.

How could they know, the first farmers,
the sowing of corn was the sowing of armed men?

I woke up
looked through the eye
of the needle of the rich
man found the view
to my taste climbed into
the tree of the knowledge
of good and evil to add
to my stature stood
in my own light admiring
my shadow and one
spoke to me there of
my one talent urging
investment the usury
of the spirit but I looked
out over the wall
of the garden where grapes grew
upon thorns and the machine gathered them and the dentures
of the children were not set on edge.

I want...Help me. Listen...I –
no time. What is life but
deciduous? That I in my day, no
other...I, I, I, before the world,
in the present tense; so, now,
here, stating my condition –
whose else? Not my fault; I
at the centre, everything else
echoes, reflections. What is water
but mirror, air but returner
of the personal cadenza I...
I...I – What is my name?
I, a pacifist, fighting in the dark-
ness against the will not to be.
There will be no peace in the world
so long as the angel resists me.

God smiled. The controls
were working: the small
eaten by the large, the large
by the larger. One problem
remained: the immunity
of a species. 'Easy,'
the jester at his side
whispered, indicating
the air's window that the germs
thronged. God opened it
a crack, and the human edifice
was dismantled. Among the ruins
one, stupider than the rest,
sat, seeing history's wheel
idle, putting a hand out, ready
to start it all over again.

There is a being, they say,
neither body nor spirit,
that is more power than reason, more reason
than love, whose origins
are unknown, who is apart
and with us, the silence
to which we appeal, the architect
of our failure. It takes the genes
and experiments with them and our children
are born blind, or seeing have
smooth hands that are the instruments
of destruction. It is the spoor
in the world's dark leading away
from the discovered victim, the expression
the sky shows us after
an excess of spleen. It has gifts it
distributes to those least fitted
to use them. It is everywhere and
nowhere, and looks sideways into the shocked face
of life, challenging it to disown it.

'As bubbles' one said,
        'in the great bowl
of the sky; they come
        into being, they endure,
they explode. As are
        the stars, so we, but
our shining goes on
        in the great memory
and time makes us again:
        the body that is our shirt
of flame is re-woven and
        we wear it for joy
that through it an identity
        can appear. Ah, love,
whose property we believe
        is to outlast the burning,
be more than mineral in us,
        more than a spark
from the bush of the imagination
        we have set on fire.'

21

Bored with it:
rock; rock eroding
to sand, a dusty
looking-glass for a god.
May as well...breathing,
leading the dust
a dance. Where did the Furies
come from, counterpointing
his music? The iron
in his mind no antidote
for anaemia of good
will. Whose was the fadeless
echo with its entreaty:
Hold my hand? Silence
was no discouragement
of its insistence. What
is a god's rest? Withdrawing
into another sphere he stared
down into the empty
womb and was engulfed by it.

# INCARNATION

Were you one of the three
came travelling to the workshop
with your gifts of heart, mind and soul
to the newly born in its cradle?

Was that a halo above it
of molecules and electrons,
with the metal gone hoarse trying
to reiterate: Holy. Holy. Holy?

You should have returned to your glass
ball, that had other futures
to betoken than the one
you became part of, a listener

to its sermons, participant
in the miracles it performed.
It was compliant, more than
accessible to your request for a sign.

> By the lake in the cool
> of the day a tumult
> like thunder. But some said:
> 'The voice of a god'
> with the promise his kingdom
> was all of this world.
> So you made sacrifice
> of your fellows, saw them torn
> upon his altars in return
> for redemption from the tyranny
> of the clock. And the cross
> that was set up was the rod
> and the crankshaft man's body
> was nailed to with no power
> to atone. And a voice
> taunted him in passing:
> 'If you were so clever
> as to invent me, come down
> now so that I may believe.'

Was there a resurrection?
Did the machine put its hand
in man's side, acknowledging lordship?

There was a third day and
a third year and the sepulchre
filled up with humanity's bones.

Was this where a god died?
Was Nietzsche correct, the smell
of oil the smell of corruption also?

On the skyline I have seen gantries
with their arms out awkwardly
as love and money trying to be reconciled.

Top left an angel
hovering. Top right the attendance
of a star. From both
bottom corners devils
look up, relishing
in prospect a divine
meal. How old at the centre
the child's face gazing
into love's too human
face, like one prepared
for it to have its way
and continue smiling?

Men go to the poll
and women to the cradle

where once the child lay
with its acorn eye

that secreted the tree
they would hang his body on.

No clouds overhead;
no troubles freckling
the maid's eye. The shadows
are immediate and are thrown

by upholstered branches,
not by that angled
event that from beyond
the horizon puts its roots

down. This is Eden
over again. The child
holds out both his hands
for the breast's apple. The snake is asleep.

BEAUTY                                    SATAN

A G E S                                      T H
 N   L                                      R U
                                           T

The Nativity? No.
Something has gone wrong.
There is a hole in the stable
acid rain drips through
onto an absence. Beauty
is hoisted upside down.
The truth is Pilate not
lingering for an answer.
The angels are prostrate
'beaten into the clay'
as Yeats thundered. Only
Satan beams down,
poisoning with fertilisers
the place where the child
lay, harrowing the ground
for the drumming of the machine-
gun tears of the rich that are
seed of the next war.

Come close. Let me whisper.
You know – the changeling
in the manger. Those limbs –
pistons. That smile
that had the polish
of the machine, lubricating
their gifts. They crucified
the wrong one – found wandering
in the country, babbling
of love and truthfulness...
no down for his bed.
While the other one made
for the town, persuading
the people; filling Calvary
with its derision; knowing
the new travellers in time
would arrive too speedily
to have grown wise on the way.

The first king was on horseback.
The second a pillion rider.
The third came by plane.

Where was the god-child?
He was in the manger
with the beasts, all looking

the other way where the fourth
was a slow dawning because
wisdom must come on foot.

Looking at it
without seeing it.
Is this the secret
of life, the masked ball

which meaning attends
incognito, as once men looked
in a manger, failing
to see the beast for the god?

Other incarnations, of course,
consonant with the environment
he finds himself in,
animating the cells,
sharpening the antennae,
becoming as they are
that they, in the transparency
of their shadows, in the filament
of their calculations, may,
in their own way, learn to confront
the intellect with its issue.

And his coming testified
to not by one star
arrested temporarily
over a Judaic manger,
but by constellations innumerable
as dew upon surfaces
he has passed over time
and again, taking to himself
the first-born of the imagination
but without the age-old requirement of blood.

I have been student of your love
and have not graduated. Setting
my own questions, I bungled
the examination: Where? Why? When?

Knowing there were no answers
you allowed history to invigilate
my desires. Time and again I was
caught with a crib up my sleeve.

# CRUCIFIXION

God's fool, God's jester
capering at his right hand
in torment, proving the fallacy
of the impassible, reminding
him of omnipotence's limits.


I have seen the figure
on our human tree, burned
into it by thought's lightning
and it writhed as I looked.


A god has no alternative
but himself. With what crown
plurality but with thorns?
Whose is the mirthless laughter
at the beloved irony
at his side? The universe over,
omniscience warns, the crosses
are being erected from such
material as is available
to remorse. What are the stars
but time's fires going out
before ever the crucified
can be taken down?
                  Today
there is only this one option
before me. Remembering,
as one goes out into space,
on the way to the sun,
how dark it will grow,
I stare up into the darkness
of his countenance, knowing it
a reflection of the three days and nights
at the back of love's looking-
glass even a god must spend.

Not the empty tomb
but the uninhabited
cross. Look long enough
and you will see the arms
put on leaves. Not a crown
of thorns, but a crown of flowers
haloing it, with a bird singing
as though perched on paradise's threshold.

We have over-furnished
our faith. Our churches
are as limousines in the procession
towards heaven. But the verities
remain: a de-nuclearised
cross, uncontaminated
by our coinage; the chalice's
ichor; and one crumb of bread
on the tongue for the bird-like
intelligence to be made tame by.

He atones not with blood
but with the transfusions
that are the substitute of its loss.

Under the arc-lamps
we suffer the kisses
of the infected needle,

satisfied to be the saviour
not of the world, not
of the species, but of the one

anonymous member
of the gambling party
at the foot of the cross.

Silent, Lord,
as you would have us be,
lips closed, eyes swerving aside
towards the equation:
$x + y^2 = y + x^2$ ?
It does not balance.
What has algebra to do
with a garden? Either
they preceded it or came
late. The snake's fangs
must have been aimed
at a calculable angle
against a possible refusal
of the apple of knowledge.
Was there a mathematics
before matter to which
you were committed? Or is it
man's mind is to blame,
spinning questions out of itself
in the infinite regress?
It is we gave the stars names,
yet already the Zodiac
was in place – prophesying,
reminding? The Plough
and Orion's Sword eternally
in contradiction. We close
our eyes when we pray
lest the curtain of tears
should come down on a cross
being used for the first time to prove
the correctness of a negation.

They set up their decoy
in the Hebrew sunlight. What
for? Did they expect
death to come sooner
to disprove his claim
to be God's son? Who
can shoot down God?
Darkness arrived at
midday, the shadow
of whose wing? The blood
ticked from the cross, but it was not
their time it kept. It was no
time at all, but the accompaniment
to a face staring,
as over twenty centuries
it has stared, from unfathomable
darkness into unfathomable light.

AD.

We must reverse our lenses.
Too often we have allowed them
to lead us into a dark past.
Looking through the right
end, we see how that dawn
had the brightness of flowers.
It is the future is dark
because one by one
we are removing these paintings
from our exhibition. We walk
between blank walls, scrawled
over with the graffiti
of a species that has turned its gaze
back in, not to discover
its incipient wings, but the slime
rather and the quagmire from which
it believes itself to have emerged.

The way the trees' boughs
intertwine, pattern of an immense
brain whose thoughts are the leaves
proliferating in April.

The way the brain resembles
a wood, impenetrable thicket
in which thought is held fast by the horns,
a sacrifice to language.

To be alive then
was to be aware how necessary
prayer was and impossible.

The philosophers had done
their work well, demolishing
proofs we never believed in.

We were drifting in space-
time, in touch with what we had
left and could not return to.

We rehearsed the excuses
for the deficiencies of love's
kingdom, avoiding our eyebeams.

Beset, as we were,
with science's signposts, we whimpered
to no purpose that we were lost.

We are here still. What
is survival's relationship
with meaning? The answer once

was the bone's music at the lips
of time. We are incinerating
them both now in the mind's crematorium.

The withholding
even of a request
that he remark my
silence: that was prayer.

I waited upon
him as a mirror
in its anonymity
waits upon absence.

Time passed. Once
from the closeness
of the invisible,
or in the after-draught

of the far-off, hurrying
about the immensity
of his being, I rose brimming
towards him like the spring-tide.

It is one of those faces
beginning to disappear
as though life were at work
with its eraser. It drizzles
at the window through which
I regard it. As one realising
its peril, it accosts me
in silence at every corner
of my indifference, appealing
to me to save it gratuitously
from extinction. There was a moment
it became dear to me, a skull
brushed by a smile as the sun
brushes a stone through ravelled
passages in the hill mist.
Must I single it with a name?
I am coming to believe,
as I age, so faithful its attendance
upon the eye's business, it is myself
I court; that this face, vague
but compelling, is a replica
of my own face hungry for meaning
at life's pane, but blearing it
over as much with my shortness
of faith as of breath.

'The body is mine and the soul is mine'
says the machine. 'I am at the dark source
where the good is indistinguishable
from evil. I fill my tanks up
and there is war. I empty them
and there is not peace. I am the sound,
not of the world breathing, but
of the catch rather in the world's breath.'

Is there a contraceptive
for the machine, that we may enjoy
intercourse with it without being overrun
by vocabulary? We go up
into the temple of ourselves
and give thanks that we are not
as the machine is. But it waits
for us outside, knowing that when
we emerge it is into the noise
of its hand beating on the breast's
iron as Pharisaically as ourselves.

It was arranged so:
An impression of nearness
contradicted by blank space.
An apparition in a tree
as of a face watching us,
changing to bark as we looked
close. For a being so large
to play hide and seek! Yet the air
drew an invisible curtain
between us and him. Coming
on his footprint in the snow
of our thought we had nothing
to measure its size by. We were
the thermometer and the barometer
of his weather, but approximate
only; what instrument could record
the pressure on us to disbelieve
when he turned cold? There were times
when, bending close over a flower,
thinking to penetrate the transparence
of its expression, we lost our footing
and fell into a presence illimitable
as its absence, descending motionlessly
in space-time, not into darkness
but into the luminosity of his shadow.

'Make my voice sharp
so it may rise to the clerestories
and pierce the ear
of the great God. And make
my sword sharp to enter
into the bowels of God's foes.'

Forget it. The Middle Ages
are over. On a bone
altar, with radiation
for candle, we make sacrifice
to the god of quasars
and pulsars, wiping
our robotic hands clean
on a disposable conscience.

But the silence in the mind
is when we live best, within
listening distance of the silence
we call God. This is the deep
calling to deep of the psalm-
writer, the bottomless ocean
we launch the armada of
our thoughts on, never arriving.

It is a presence, then,
whose margins are our margins;
that calls us out over our
own fathoms. What to do
but draw a little nearer to
such ubiquity by remaining still?

Lord of the molecule and the atom
are you Lord of the gene, too?

An ancestor mingled his sperm
with the ovum and here is a warped life.

Were they so wrong who thought, when
it thundered, you were in a rage?

What is it, when the sky twitches
with lightning, but mimicry of your grimace?

I have seen the jay, that singer
out of tune, helping itself

to a morsel out of the lark's nest,
and you beamed down imperturbably as the sun.

We are used by the bacteria.
I have known the Chattertons and the Keats'

acting as porters of their obscene luggage.
What makes you God but the freedom

you have given us to bellow our defiance
at you over the grave's maw, or to let

silence ensue so deliberately
as to be taken for an Amen.

Under the Pharaohs it was power;
backs broke under the stones
for galleries where the mice play.

At Delphi the power shifted
to the mind that gave uncomfortable
answers to its own questions.

In Judaea it was the beginning
of an ability to play blind
for tall stakes at the foot of the cross.

Leonardo possessed it,
but the price to be paid
was that the smile of his Madonna

was a reflection of the smile
on the countenance of the machine
he was in adultery with.

You show me two faces,
that of a flower opening
and of a fist contracting
like the gripping of ice.

You speak to me with two
voices, one thundering
on the ear's drum, the other
one mistakeable for silence.

Father, I said, domesticating
an enigma; and as though
to humour me you came.
But there are precipices

within you. Mild and dire,
now and absent, like us but
wholly other – which side
of you am I to believe?

He is that great void
we must enter, calling
to one another on our way
in the direction from which
he blows. What matter
if we should never arrive
to breed or to winter
in the climate of our conception?

Enough we have been given wings
and a needle in the mind
to respond to his bleak north.

There are times even at the Pole
when he, too, pauses in his withdrawal
so that it is light there all night long.

Tricyano-aminopropene –
it is our new form
of prayer, with biological
changes as an Amen.

Nothing is outside
God. We have attributed
violence to him. Why not
implicate him in injections?

There is an invisible
soil that we grow in.
Supposing, down at our roots,
we began taking in

minerals of non-violence,
measuring our development
by the conditioned photosynthesis
of an inward light.

They will come to understand
our folk-tale was the machine.
We listened to it in the twilight
of our reason, taking it as the hour

in which truth dawned. They will return
without moving to an innocence
as in advance of their knowledge
as the smile of the Christ child was of its cross.

On an evening like this
the furies have receded.
There are only the shining sentinels
at hand: Yeats in his tower,
who was his own candle,
poring over the manuscript
of his people, discovering pride
in defeat; discovering the lidless
eye that beholds the beast
and the virgin. Edward Llwyd,
finding the flower that grew
nowhere but in Wales,
teaching us to look for rare things
in high places. Owain Glyndŵr
who tried blowing that flower
into flame in the memory
of an oppressed nation. The poets,
all of them, in all languages,
pausing on their migration
between thought and word
to watch here with me now
the moon come to its fifteenth phase
from whose beauty and madness
men have withdrawn these last days,
hand on heart, to its far
side of sanity and darkness.

Beauty is ill
and has a drawn
face. The machine is everywhere
and is young. How can I
find God? Out there?
He is absent. In here?
He is dumb. Everywhere
there is confetti,
but there are no vows
kept. Nature submits
to concrete and macadam
that are the lava
pouring from the eruption
of the species. The power
to help is unequal
to the consciousness
of the need. Who am I?
the commodities ask
our vocabulary, outdistancing
it, on their way where?

There must be the mountain
receiving its degree
in purple and ermine;

and the girl with the drained face
moving the beholder
to ecstasy and grief.

There must be the skull
with spectacles on it
seeing what none see,

and the fly in the web
with its decibels of music
not attained to before.

All these must be there
as so many threads
of the garment without seam.

And to enthral the journey
that has no ending, once in a while
the falling of his shadow.

Madness? Its power
is to be recognised by the sane.
The insane ignore it.

They are busy with shells,
flowers, the difficulty
of discovering whose face it is

grimacing at them in the mirror.
There is no certainty
that we die when we are dead.

Maybe Dante was right;
maybe hell is inversion,
the becoming an inmate

of the paradise of the insane.
Manacled with equations,
foaming poetry at the mouth,

we will stare through the bones' bars
at those staring in, doing the mind's
trick over and over again to amuse them.

The imperatives of the instincts
in abeyance, heart and mind
at one in their contemplation
of the ripening apple never

to fall from the topmost branches
of truth's tree. A site for the repair
of promises that were broken, for picking
up pieces of the smashed dream.

It has the freshness of mushrooms,
proof of the whiteness darkness
can bring forth. It is the timeless
place, the unaccommodated

moment; an interval in the performance
of an unheard music. Do not believe
those who have been everywhere
but here. Tell the poor of the world

there is nothing to pay, no distance
to travel; that they are invited
to the marriage of here and now;
that the crystal in which they look,

grey with foreboding as the moon
with earth's shadow, has this
as its far side, turning necessarily towards
us with the reversal of our values.

When we are weak, we are
strong. When our eyes close
on the world, then somewhere
within us the bush

burns. When we are poor
and aware of the inadequacy
of our table, it is to that
uninvited the guest comes.

I think that maybe
I will be a little surer
of being a little nearer.
That's all. Eternity
is in the understanding
that that little is more than enough.

**R.S. Thomas** was born in 1913 in Cardiff, and now lives in Gwynedd. He won the Heinemann Award in 1955, the Queen's Gold Medal for Poetry in 1964, and the Cholmondeley Award in 1978, and has received the Welsh Arts Council's literature award three times.

He has published twenty books of poems since his first collection *The Stones of the Field* appeared in 1946, including *Selected Poems 1946-1968*, published by Bloodaxe, and its sequel *Later Poems 1972-1982* from Macmillan, publishers of his recent collections *Experimenting with an Amen* (1986) and *The Echoes Return Slow* (1988). Seren Books have published two other collections, *Ingrowing Thoughts* (1985) and *Welsh Airs* (1987), as well as his *Selected Prose* (1983) and *Critical Writings on R.S. Thomas* (1983). His autobiography, *Neb*, written in Welsh, was published by Gwasg Gwynedd in 1985.